SUPER SIMPLE BODY

INSIDE THE EARS

KARIN HALVORSON, M.D.

Consulting Editor, Diane Craig, M.A./Reading Specialist

A Division of ABDO

ABDO
Publishing Company

VISIT US AT WWW.ABDOPUBLISHING.COM

Published by ABDO Publishing Company, a division of
ABDO, P.O. Box 398166, Minneapolis, Minnesota 55439.
Copyright © 2013 by Abdo Consulting Group, Inc.
International copyrights reserved in all countries. No
part of this book may be reproduced in any form without
written permission from the publisher. Super SandCastle™
is a trademark and logo of ABDO Publishing Company.

Printed in the United States of America,
North Mankato, Minnesota
102012
012013

 PRINTED ON RECYCLED PAPER

Editor: Liz Salzmann
Content Developer: Nancy Tuminelly
Cover and Interior Design: Anders Hanson, Mighty Media
Photo Credits: Shutterstock, Dorling Kindersley RF/Thinkstock,
Colleen Dolphin

Library of Congress Cataloging-in-Publication Data
Halvorson, Karin, 1979-
 Inside the ears / Karin Halvorson ; consulting editor, Diane Craig.
   p. cm. -- (Super simple body)
 ISBN 978-1-61783-610-7
 1. Ear--Juvenile literature. 2. Hearing--Juvenile literature. I. Title.
 QP462.2.H36 2013
 612.8'5--dc23
                          2012028770

Super SandCastle™ books are created by a team of professional
educators, reading specialists, and content developers around five
essential components—phonemic awareness, phonics, vocabulary,
text comprehension, and fluency—to assist young readers as they
develop reading skills and strategies and increase their general
knowledge. All books are written, reviewed, and leveled for guided
reading, early reading intervention, and Accelerated Reader®
programs for use in shared, guided, and independent reading
and writing activities to support a balanced approach to literacy
instruction.

NOTE TO ADULTS

THIS BOOK is all about encouraging
children to learn the science of how
their bodies work! Be there to help
make science fun and interesting for
young readers. Many activities are
included in this book to help children
further explore what they've learned.
Some require adult assistance and/
or permission. Make sure children have
appropriate places where they can do
the activities safely.

Children may also have questions about
what they've learned. Offer help and
guidance when they have questions.
Most of all encourage them to keep
exploring and learning new things!

CONTENTS

YOUR BODY

YOUR EARS

You're amazing! So is your body!

Your body has a lot of different parts. Your eyes, ears, brain, stomach, lungs, and heart all work together every day. They keep you moving. Even when you don't realize it.

When you listen to your favorite song or talk to your friends, your ears are working. They turn **vibrations** in the air into sounds you can hear!

Ears also help you balance. Without your ears, it would be hard to walk and run!

CAN YOU THINK OF OTHER WAYS THAT YOU USE YOUR EARS?

ALL ABOUT THE
EAR

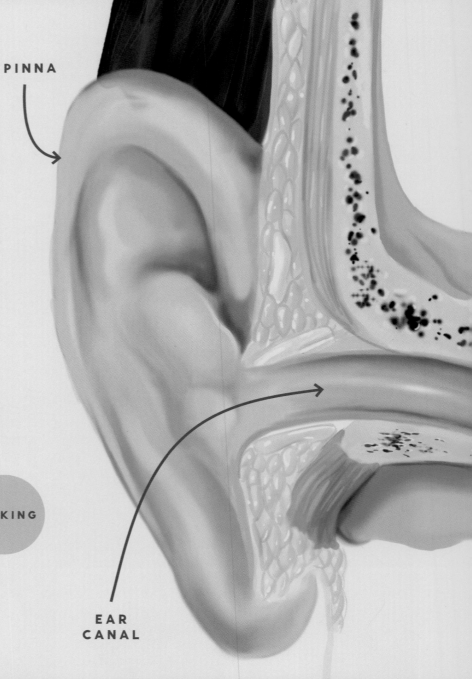

PINNA

Your ears capture sounds. Then they direct the sounds into your head. They are like funnels for sound!

MUSIC

TALKING

NOISES

EAR CANAL

Ears have a lot of tiny parts that you can't see. That's because they're inside your head! They work together so you can hear!

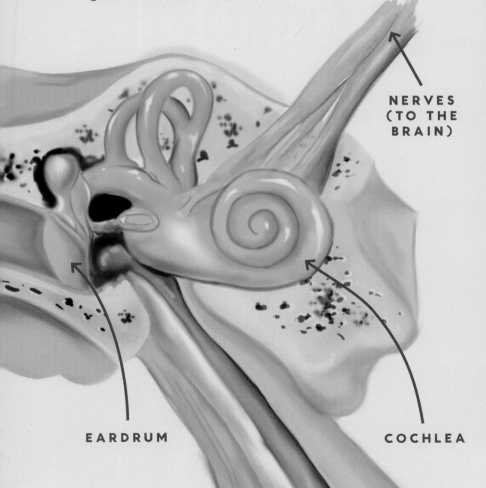

NERVES (TO THE BRAIN)

EARDRUM

COCHLEA

WHAT IS SOUND?

Sound comes from **vibrations** in the air. Your ears capture those vibrations. Your ears change the vibrations into signals that your brain can understand. Then you can hear them!

Vibrations in the air can't be seen. Wind is a good example of an air vibration. How do you know when it's windy? You can't see it. But you can feel it on your body. You can also hear it!

HEAR YE, HEAR YE

WHAT CAN YOU HEAR?

WHAT YOU NEED: PAPER, CHAIR, TAPE, MEASURING TAPE, A FRIEND, OPEN SPACE

HOW TO DO IT

1. Sit in a chair. Have a friend stand behind you 25 steps away. Then your friend walks slowly toward you. With each step, your friend snaps his or her fingers.

2. Raise your hand when you can hear the snap. Your friend marks that spot on the floor with tape.

3. Roll the paper into a cone. Use tape to make sure it stays rolled. Repeat steps 1 and 2. This time put the small end of the cone in your ear.

4. Measure the distance between the two pieces of tape. Did it take fewer steps for you to hear the snap using the cone?

WHAT'S HAPPENING?

Your ear is shaped like a cone to funnel sound into your ear. The cone acts like a bigger funnel. It brings even more sound into your ear.

ALL EARS!

Your ears each have three parts. They are the **outer** ear, the middle ear, and the **inner** ear. Sounds pass through them on their way to your brain.

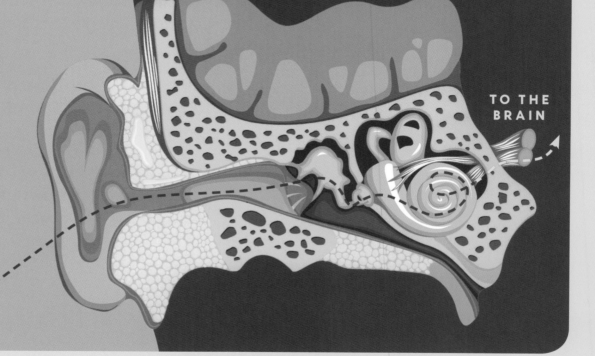

TO THE BRAIN

SOUND

OUTER EAR

MIDDLE EAR

INNER EAR

Human ears can sense a range of sounds. Some sounds are outside that range. They are too high or too low for us to hear.

Pitch is how high or low a sound is. It depends on how fast the sound **vibrates**. The faster it vibrates, the higher the pitch.

Many animals can hear a larger range of pitches than humans. Dogs can hear sounds that are too high-pitched for people to hear.

PICTURING VIBRATIONS

Sound vibrations can be pictured as wavy lines. The more waves in the line, the higher the pitch!

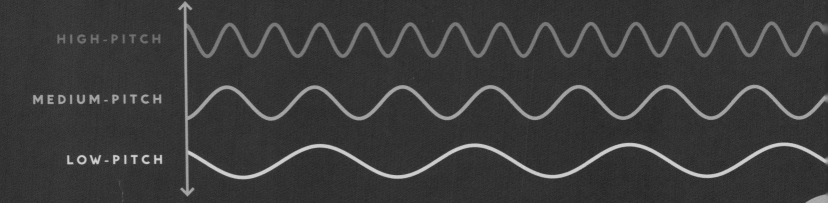

HIGH-PITCH

MEDIUM-PITCH

LOW-PITCH

THE
EAR YOU SEE

Part of your ear is *inside* your head. But when people say *ear*, they're usually talking about the part that's *outside* your head. That's the part that people can see! It's called the pinna (**PIN-UH**).

People pierce their pinnae to wear earrings. They are where you put earmuffs and headphones.

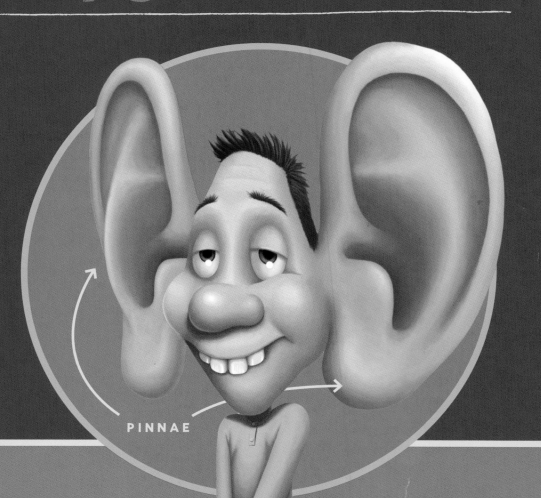

PINNAE

The pinna does three things to help you hear.

First, the pinna catches sounds, like a net!

Then it filters the sounds. This makes it easier to hear voices.

Finally, the pinna funnels the sounds into your ear canal.

EARWAX TO THE MAX!

Do you ever find sticky or flaky stuff in your ears? That's earwax. It has several important jobs.

It keeps your ear canals MOIST. This keeps your ears from getting **itchy**.

It has bacteria that help PREVENT EAR INFECTIONS.

It COLLECTS DUST AND DIRT so the middle ear stays clean.

Sometimes people have too much earwax. It can be removed. But NEVER STICK ANYTHING IN YOUR EAR. Have an adult do it for you.

TIN CAN TELEPHONE

CAN YOU HEAR ME NOW?

WHAT YOU NEED: TWO EMPTY TIN CANS OR PLASTIC CUPS, SOAP, WATER, PLIERS, HAMMER, LARGE NAIL, 12 FEET (3.6 M) OF STRING, A FRIEND

HOW TO DO IT

1 Take the tops off the tin cans. Clean the tin cans with soap and water. Use pliers to push down any sharp edges.

2 Use the hammer and nail to make a hole in the bottom of each can. Have an adult help with this.

3 Put the ends of the string up through the holes in the cans. Tie knots in the ends of the string. Make sure the knots can't fit through the holes.

4 You and your friend each hold a can. Stand far enough apart so the string is tight. Have your friend hold the can over his or her ear. Hold your can over your mouth and say something. Did your friend hear you? Take turns talking and listening.

WHAT'S HAPPENING?

When you talk into your can, the can **vibrates**. The string carries the **vibrations** to the other can. This makes your friend's can vibrate the way yours did. It recreates the sound of your voice!

VIBRATIONS

Sound **vibrations** enter the ear canal. At the end of the ear canal, they hit the eardrum. The eardrum is a thin wall of muscle and skin. The eardrum stretches tightly across the ear canal. It's like the skin of a drum.

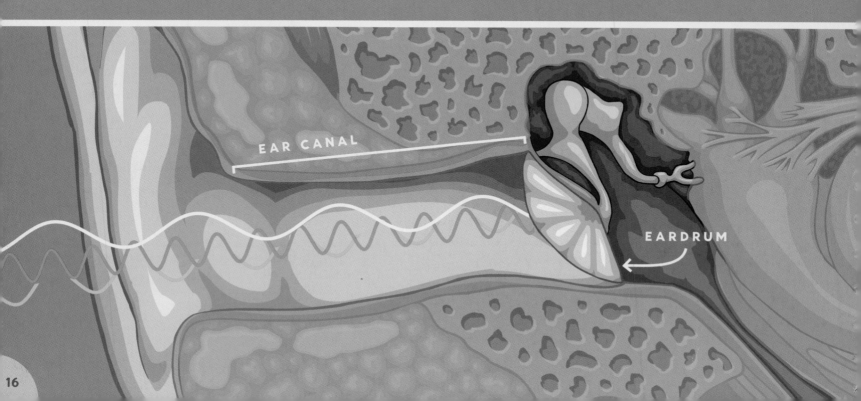

EAR CANAL

EARDRUM

When you hit a drum, it **vibrates**. Eardrums work the same way. When **vibrations** hit the eardrum, it vibrates too!

POPPING EARS

Sometimes air gets trapped behind your eardrum. It can happen when you go up or down very fast.

There is a tube from your middle ear to your nose. It can open to let air out. This often happens when you **yawn** or swallow. You hear a popping sound. Then the pain goes away because the air is gone.

PLAY IT BY EAR

BANG THE DRUM!

WHAT YOU NEED: LARGE BOWL, PLASTIC WRAP, LARGE RUBBER BAND, 1 TABLESPOON OF UNCOOKED RICE, MEASURING SPOON, METAL PIE PAN, WOODEN SPOON

HOW TO DO IT

1. Put plastic wrap over the top of the bowl. Pull it tight. Put the rubber band around the outside of the bowl. Make sure it is over the plastic wrap.

2. Put the uncooked rice on the plastic wrap.

3. Hold the pie pan near the bowl. Tap a beat on the pan with the wooden spoon. Watch what happens! Try moving the pan farther from the bowl. How far away are you when the rice stops jumping?

WHAT'S HAPPENING?

When you hit the pie pan, it **vibrates**. The **vibration** travels through the air. When the vibration reaches the plastic wrap, it vibrates too! That makes the rice jump. The plastic wrap acts like your eardrum.

FEEL IT IN
YOUR BONES

The eardrum sends sound **vibrations** to the middle ear. The middle ear has three small bones. They are the malleus (MAL-EE-UHS), the incus (ING-KUHS), and the stapes (STAY-PEEZ). Together they are called the ossicles (AH-SI-KUHLZ). The ossicles send the sound vibrations on to your **inner** ear. They also make sounds louder.

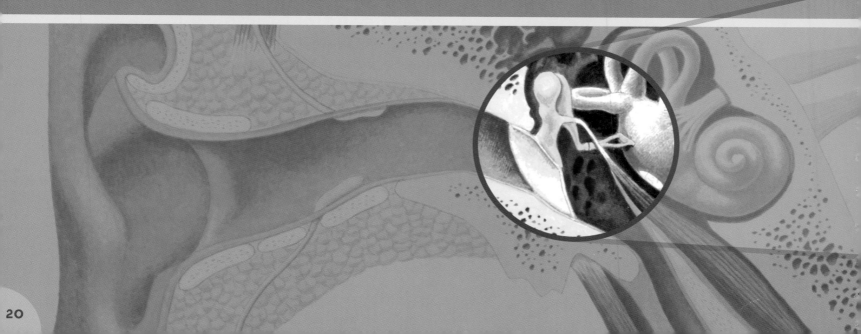

The eardrum is connected to the malleus. The malleus presses against the incus. And the incus connects to the stapes. Sound **vibrations** travel through each bone on the way to the **inner** ear.

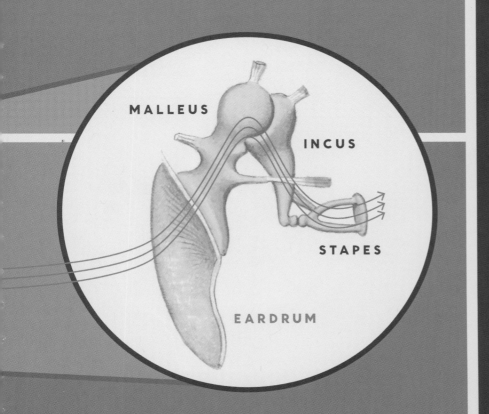

MALLEUS

INCUS

STAPES

EARDRUM

IT'S TOO LOUD!

When a sound is too loud, your ears flex their muscles!

Tiny muscles keep the ossicles from moving too much. So less sound reaches your inner ear.

{ FAST FACT }

THE OSSICLES ARE THE
THREE SMALLEST BONES
IN YOUR BODY!

EXPLORATION

The **inner** ear has a small tube called the cochlea (KOH-KLEE-UH). It's smaller than a pea! The cochlea is shaped like a snail's shell.

The cochlea is filled with water. It has an opening called the oval window.

The oval window is covered by a thin membrane. The stapes sits on top of it. When the stapes **vibrates**, the membrane vibrates. That makes the water inside the cochlea move.

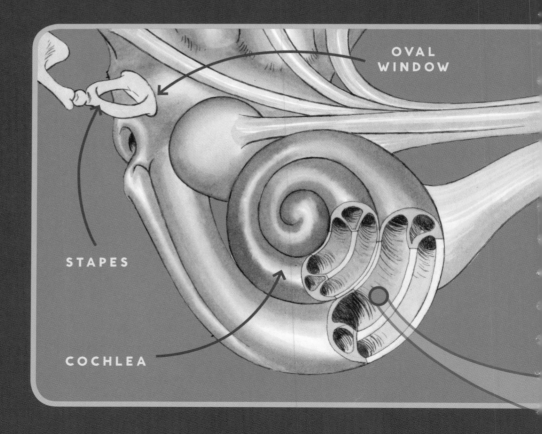

OVAL WINDOW

STAPES

COCHLEA

HAIR-RAISING

SOUNDS

The cochlea is lined with tiny hair cells. When the water inside the cochlea moves, the hair cells move too. The moving hair cells brush against **nerves**. The nerves send signals to the brain.

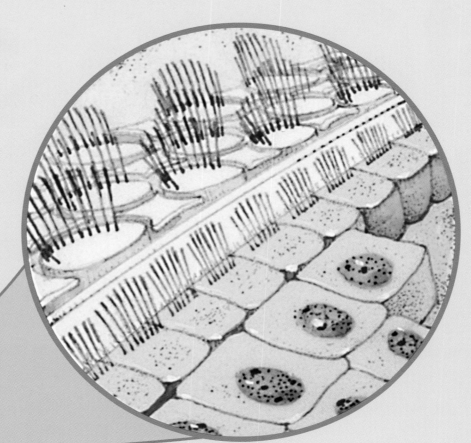

MUSIC TO MY EARS

OF SOUND AND STRINGS

WHAT YOU NEED: 2 FEET OF STRING (61 CM), SPOON, 2 PAPER CUPS, PENCIL, DESK OR TABLE

HOW TO DO IT

1. Tie the string around the spoon. The spoon should be in the middle of the string.

2. Poke a hole in the bottom of each paper cup with a pencil.

3. Put the ends of the string up through the holes in the cups. Tie knots in the ends of the string. Make sure the knots can't fit through the holes.

4. Hold a cup in each hand. Swing the spoon so it hits the desk. This makes the spoon **vibrate**. Did you hear a sound?

5. Put the cups over your ears. Swing the spoon against the desk again. What did you hear this time?

WHAT'S HAPPENING?

The spoon made the same noise both times. The first time it traveled through the air to your ears. The second time it went through the string. The string vibrated like the hair cells in your ears.

IN A
DIZZY TIZZY

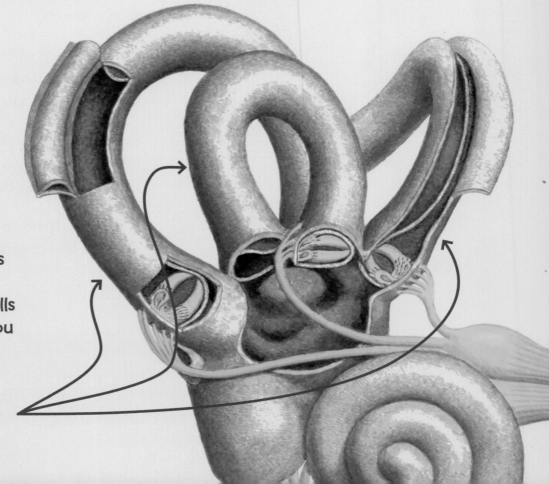

There are three tubes next to the cochlea. They look like loops! They're called the **semicircular** canals. They help you balance.

The canals have water in them. When you move, the water in the canals moves too. Hair cells inside the canals tell your brain about the movement. Then your brain tells your muscles what to do so you don't fall over.

SEMICIRCULAR CANALS

Sometimes your brain gets tricked. Try spinning around and then suddenly stop. The water in your **semicircular** canals keeps moving. Your brain thinks that you're still moving. But you're not. That's why you get **dizzy**!

FOR THE EARS!

Nerves connect your **inner** ear to your brain. They send electric signals to the brain. The signals tell the brain about **vibrations** in your ears. That's how you understand what you hear!

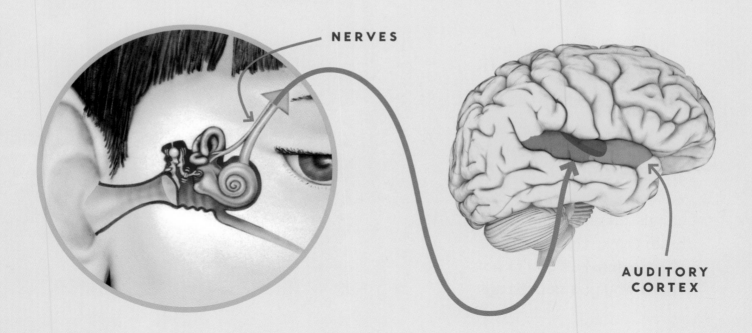

NERVES

AUDITORY CORTEX

WHY DO YOU HAVE TWO?

You have two ears so that you can tell where a sound is coming from.

Your ears are on opposite sides of your head. The distance between them causes each ear to hear sounds a little differently. Your brain uses the differences to tell where the sound is coming from. It can also tell how far away the sound is.

WHAT SOUNDS CAN YOU LOCATE?

MAKE YOUR OWN EAR

SHOW WHAT YOU'VE LEARNED!

WHAT YOU NEED: SPRINGFORM PAN, SCISSORS, RUBBER BAND, PLASTIC WRAP, CARDSTOCK, RULER, BENDABLE STRAW, TAPE, PING-PONG BALL, LARGE BOWL, WATER

HOW TO DO IT

1. Remove the bottom of the springform pan. Cover the top of the pan with plastic wrap. Use a rubber band to hold it in place. Make sure the plastic wrap is tight. Set the pan on its side. This is the eardrum.

2. Cut a triangle out of cardstock. Each side should be 3 inches (7.6 cm) long. Fold the triangle in half. Tape the long end of the bendable straw to one side of the triangle. The straw is like the ossicles. Tape the ping-pong ball to the other end of the straw.

3. Tape the other side of the triangle to the middle of the plastic wrap. Place a bowl of water in front of the pan. Set the ping-pong ball on the water. The ping-pong ball and water are like the cochlea.

4. Clap near the eardrum. Watch the ball move up and down.

WHAT'S HAPPENING?

You made a model of your ear! It shows how your ear works. When your eardrum moves, the water in your cochlea moves too!

DIZZY – having a whirly, unsteady feeling.

INFECTION – a disease caused by the presence of bacteria or other germs.

INNER – on the inside.

ITCH – an irritating or bothersome feeling on the skin.

NERVE – one of the threads in the body that take messages to and from the brain.

OUTER – on the outside.

SEMICIRCULAR – shaped like half of a circle.

VIBRATE – to move rapidly back and forth.

VIBRATION – the act of moving rapidly back and forth.

YAWN – to open one's mouth very wide and breathe deeply.

GLOSSARY